Grandma's Poems

written by Shirley Summers

About the author

I was born in Tacoma, Washington and lived here all my life. I worked for the telephone company retired after 36 years service. I started writing poems in my 80's. It was a God given gift. I lost my two children in my 80's so God knew I needed something to get me through the lonely days and lonely nights. God got my brain working, now I'm writing poems. Never give up, we never know what tomorrow will bring.

About the book designer

My name is Sandra Moreano and I am an Artist and Book Designer. I help artist and storytellers create and market their own books. Some are just for family and some are sold on the internet. I help in every stage of the process.

Table of Contents

Seasons

Fantasy

Holidays

Life Lessons

Two Little Robins

Two little robins gathered twigs and sticks.

To build a little love nest for their future chicks.

They lived outside my window

so I watched in pure delight

how the Mama and Papa

sat on tiny eggs many days and nights.

Finally three little chicks were hatched.

It was a miracle to see,

Now I hear the songs from the birdies in the trees.

First three tiny eggs then three baby chicks.

Then young robins in the sky.

Life's a mystery from the cradle

till we die.

The Flood

A pair of all God's creatures marching two by two.
Down to the arc like they were told to do
There were elephants and monkeys and kangaroos
Cats and dogs and creepy things too
Noah was waiting, kneeling and praying
That God would see them through
Soon the rain came down
There was flooding all around
Forty days and forty nights this all went on
Finally the dove came calling
the rain stopped falling
And there was land in view
They all went ashore so merrily
To start all life anew.

Little Clown

There was a little clown
who would go from town to town
just to make the people laugh
In so many cases
he would find tears upon some faces
And that should never last
So he'd do his little act
He'd pull an old stuffed rabbit from a hat
This would make them laugh,
Then he's stop to say
Jesus loves you everyday
And that's what really matters anyway.

Love is Here to Stay

Love is like a warm warm blanket
when the weather is 32 degrees
But love can make you mad
Or love and make you sad
Or fill your heart with glee
So be kind and faithful
So love can grow and grow
Love is like flowers in the garden
You must feed and weed it as you go
So live and love to the fullest
And enjoy each waking day
God wants us to be happy
So love is here to stay.

Happier Days Ahead

When unhappy days comes drifting by
don't run away and hide
the sun will come again someday
take time to cry
take time to pray
and let the lord come in.

Stick and Stones

Don't say
sticks and stones can break your bones
But names will never hurt you
You're fat, you're dumb, will stick like gum.
Don't say something to hurt some one.
The names you say never go away
They live forever after
Try to say something kind each day
To bring some joy and laugher.

Jimmy and King

There was a little dog
Hungry and all alone
There was a little boy
Wanting a dog to love
and call his own.

They met.
It was love at first sight
So Jimmy took the doggy home.
Mom and dad were happy too
Cause love and happiness just grew and grew.
King would wait for Jim each day
Cause after school they'd romp and play.
Years of love brought love and joy
To a faithful old dog
And a teenage boy.

Animals

Little Benny

My little dog Benny lights up my life
He's my little companion morning and night
Benny loves when we walk in the park
Or rides in my old Chevrolet
With the window's rolled down
So he can look all around
to see what he can see
And if I need a friend I can depend on my Ben
He's never too far away
The love that he shows
Is more precious than gold.
It brings love and happiness to me.

Little Cuddles

My little dog Cuddles
is as sweet as can be
She looks all around,
she's looking for me
She's up on my lap
Wanting my love
She gives me wet kisses
And that's ok too
because friends like my Cuddles
are so far and so few.

My little Cat Tootsie

My little cat Tootsie
Is an independent cat
She loves to sit by the window and take long napes
Sometimes when I call her it's only in vain
Seems many times she doesn't know her name
But when she sits on my lap
Snuggles and purrs
I know Tootsie love me
And I love her.

The cat and the mouse

There was a little mouse in a house on a hill.
He would get into all kinds of mischief
when everything was still.
No one could catch the little mouse in a trap.
He was much smarter than that .
So the next thing to do was to get a mean cat.
Fur was flying the little mouse was crying .
He looked at the cat and asked,
 "Why hurt me? I'll do you no harm."
So they kissed and made up and ran to the barn.
The joke was on dad.
No more patience he had.
He was at his wits end
because the cat and the mouse
became really good friends.

Three little squirrels

Three little squirrels high in the trees
A mama and papa and baby makes three
They gather and bury food all year
Cause food can be scarce when winter is here
I understand why they do all of this
No welfare, no food stamps to help them exist
So please animal lovers let's help them survive
Put out some food for those cute little guys.

All Creatures

I love all the creatures in this big wide world

Mr. Alligator and the big mouth toad

The monkeys and the donkeys

The cats and the rats

Thank-you Noah for getting in the act

God Bless all creatures big, tall, and small

You bring much happiness I love and enjoy you all

Life Span

My little grandson Dennis

My little grandson Dennis
Lives next door
He's grandmother's little sweetheart
He's only four
He likes to go fishing with grandpa and me
And he likes watching cartoons on our TV
He likes me to read stories to him
He listens and listens
Till the sandman drops in
I love baking cookies for my sweet little boy
By now you must know he's my
Pride and joy

Youth

Youth, you grow up too fast
There's lots at stake
Think twice, three times
You'll make mistakes
You'll try to smoke,
Then a beer or two
Don't' try the drugs they will ruin you.
First get your education
Then get yourself a job
Life will be much sweeter
if you make your parents
proud.

Johnny's Happy Childhood

Little Johnny was so happy
In his home upon the hill
Where love just seemed to grow and grow and
Never did stand still
His dad would go to work each day
And mom would care for John
Every week there was some pay
To help them carry on
Johnny's mom and dad made time for family fun
No wonder Johnny grew to be that loving son.

Sweet Sixteen

When I was sweet sixteen
My driver's license was my big dream
At 21 I met and married a nice young man
10 months later we were mom and dad
to the sweetest little gal
and a handsome little lad
At 42 I had an empty nest
that's not the best
So I got a good job
made lots of friends
Soon my career was coming to an end
Now I'm 62 sitting on my deck
relaxing and waiting for my SS check
Life is good.

I know why Papa said No

When I was just a little lad
I would ask my dad
Can we go fishing just you and me?
Maybe catch a big one, mama would be pleased
Or papa can we go camping out in the woods
It will be fun and food tastes so good
Or papa can we go to a Seahawks game
We'll eat hot dogs and ice cream
And yell for our team
Most of the time papa would say
I'm ready son, don't you delay
At 17 I asked to borrow the car
Not to go far
Papa said NO
Now I'm a dad with a lad of my own
Now I understand why papa said no.

Life's Kiss

When you're in love you're on cloud nine
Soon the wedding bells will chime
Someday a family there will be
You're excited
You are pleased
But kids don't stay kids for very long
They grow too fast and then they're gone
Just wait awhile and you will see
A little grandchild on your knee
A little one to love and hold
A happy thought when you grow old
When I start to reminisce
I have to smile
And I'll admit that this first started with a kiss.

Old Age

When I look in the mirror
I see an old face
I remember seeing a young gal
Dressed in gingham or lace
Getting ready for work
Or for a hot date
Where did time go?
I really don't know
Old age is a pain
I hate to complain
But thank heavens for
Doctors, walkers, wheelchairs, and canes

Old Age 2

If I was 50 years younger
I'd get a little dog
One sweet and cuddly
and not mean at all
I'd go on a diet and get real lean
I'd get a new car and
Tight fitting jeans
But since I'm not young any longer
But older indeed
I'll rock in my rocker
And dream all those dreams

Not too particular

The man was feeling all alone
He wanted someone to call his own
A blue eyed blond with curly hair
Or a red headed gal with skin so fair
Or a pretty brunette would surely do
He's not too particular
He's 92

Seasons

Spring has Come

Friend

A walk in the Woods

I drove and I drove

Summertime

At the Beach

Let it Rain

Autumn

Winter is Coming

Spring has come

Spring has come, oh glory be
Bringing pretty little daffodils and budding trees
Things begin to come alive
There's running nose and watery eyes
There grass to mow and gardens to hoe
But the sun is shining
And the fish are biting
Let's grab a pole and away we go
Down to the nearest fishing hole.

Friend

When the morning sun is shinning
and the dew still on the ground
what a pleasant way to start the day
and you know that later on
a friend you'll meet,
a bit to eat
perhaps a walk
and lots and lots of girly talk
and when the day has ended
and you go your separate ways
your happy and contented
to have spent the day that way
with a friend.

A walk in the woods

Let's go for a walk in the woods
Where the air is so fresh and so good
The sky is so blue
And the sun shining through
There are birds in the trees
And squirrels running free
Let's grab a blanket and food
And have a picnic for two
Just me and you
Out in the woods.

I drove and I drove

It was a hot summer day
I got in my old Chevrolet
And I drove and I drove
Many miles away
Down to the beach where the waters run deep
There were children at play
Birds in the trees
And squirrels running free
I looked all around
A mountain I found all covered with snow
The sun out to please
And the gentle sea breeze made happiness flow
I left with a smile as big as the miles I drove
My next trip will be
back with the seagulls
down by the sea.

Summertime

It's summertime
I open my blinds and what do I see?
Flowers and squirrels and birds in the trees
And old Mr. sun shining down from above
Spreading warmth and comfort joy and love
I waited all winter for summer to come
So I'll grab my bikini
And my 4 legged sweetie
And away we will run
Down to the beach for some fun in the sun.

At the Beach

It's so nice when summer is here
You head for the beach
You pack up some beer
A blanket or two a book by your side
Sun lotion, sunglasses and a big towel to dry
It warmed up so quickly
I'll go for a swim
I'll test the waters,
I'll stick my toes in
I'm up to my ankles but the water's too cold
So back to my blanket to warm up my toes.

Let it Rain

Summer is here

That means baseball, hotdogs, and cold cold beer

There's hiking and biking and camping out too

There's fishing and golfing maybe a trip to the zoo

So many fun things for people to do

But sometimes it gets too dry and too hot

That you can fry an egg on any old rock

Then it's time for a change

Let it rain, let it rain, let it rain.

Autumn

Autumn is here and oh what a sight
God painted the trees and what a delight
The trees are so gorgeous they are crimson and gold
The big harvest moon is so bright and so bold
Beauty surrounds us all through the year
Take time to enjoy when autumn is here.

Winter is Coming

Winter is coming flowers fade away leaves will fall

Winter is on its way in spite of it all

Birds fly south when winter is here

But life will return in the spring of the year

Flowers bloom again, Leaves appear

Birds return

When winter disappears.

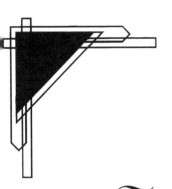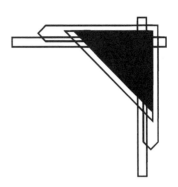

Fantasy

I'm an Old Oak Tree

I'm a little Car

Mickey and Minnie

Prince Charming

Minnie the Mermaid

Lady Luck

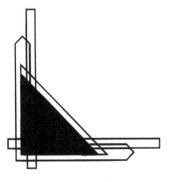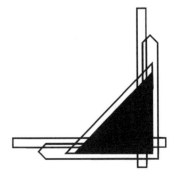

I'm an old oak tree

I'm an old oak tree

And I have a story to tell

About a family I loved and knew so well

There was Susie Mae and little Jim,

Their papa made a treehouse and swing for them

They would stay and play all day

Till their parents called them in

They had a little dog named Tim

He was calm and cool till the kids came home
from school

Then he would run and play and join the fun

The kids grew up and moved away

But they come home on holidays

They look and smile and point my way

I know they still remember the good times

We spend together

Just me and Susie Mae,

Jim and little Tim

I'm a little car

I'm a little car
I've traveled near and far
Over hills and over dales
Busy highways and country trails
Tell me why do people drive so fast
If they're caught it means big cash
And why do people drink and drive?
Don't they want to stay alive?
And why do people drive so near?
I had to stop, one hit my rear
Now I'm in the body shop
The other car is dead as rocks

Mickey and Minnie

Mickey and Minnie are a delightful pair
They sing and they dance and they go everywhere
You feel like a kid when the two are around
There's smiles on all faces
No room for a frown
There's love and laughter wherever they go
The world is much nicer it takes on a glow
So thank-you Mickey and Minnie and old Goofy too
You bring much happiness,
you chase away blues.

Prince Charming

I was walking down an old crooked road
I kept noticing a little old toad
I bent down to see why he kept following me
He looked me in the eye
He wasn't shy and said
I have a plan I want to be your man
Oh no, oh yes, just wait and see there's magic about me
And he changed from a toad to a man
He was rich and handsome with a body so lean
But then I awoke
Oh what a joke
Prince Charming was only a dream

Minnie the Mermaid

Minnie the Mermaid is so prim and so proper
She swims all around in the bay.
All the fisherman who see her
adore her.
She smiles, waves goodbye
swims away.
Old Barnacle Bill thought he'd woo her.
He planted a kiss on her face.
To his surprise she swam out of sight
and that was the end of Bill's date

Lady Luck

If I would win the lotto
I'll tell you what I'd do
I'd fix up my little old house
And make it look like new
I'd junk my old jalopy
And get a brand new car
One I could depend on
To take me near or far
And I have some friends and relatives
That need a little help
Then I'd bank the rest
For my little, old, aching self
So please lady luck
Don't hesitate
If it doesn't happen quickly
It might be too late
Remember I'm eighty eight

Holidays

My Valentine

When it's St. Patty's Day

Pat and Mike

Easter Bunny

The 4th of July

Halloween

Thanksgiving

Rudolph-Tiny Snowflaks

No child should hear

Santa gets stuck

What every Child should hear

New Year's Eve

My Valentine

I over heard my papa say
Today is Valentine's Day
The coffee all made
Ready for my sweetheart and my best friend too
I'm a lucky fellow to have a wife like you
I remember when we first met
You had the cutest little wiggle
And the sweetest little giggle
And a smile I'll never forget
It was 40 years ago today
That the preacher heard us say I do
I wouldn't change you for the world
I'm more in love with you.

When it's St. Patty's Day

When it's St. Patty's Day
All the little leprechauns come out to play
Where do they go?
Out where the shamrocks grow
What do they do?
They gig and sing and
Do lots of fun things
What do little leprechauns eat?
Corn beef and cabbage and green beer to drink
When the day is over and the moon in high
They'll kiss the blarney stone, then wave goodbye
I hope next year they'll come again
Cause I'll be waiting for my little friends

Pat and Mike

Pat and Mike were the best of friends
They met at O'Reilly's Inn
They were honest and true
And hard workers too
Anyone would be proud to be kin
The two fell in love
A marriage there was
For Michael O'Shay and Miss Patty May
And I'm proud to say
I'm Danny O'Shay
I'm Pat and Mike's freckled face kid

Easter Bunny

Mr. Easter Bunny
Speaks to Mrs. Hen
He asks if she has eggs to spare
And tells her of his plan

I color and hide Easter eggs
for kids throughout the land
And I love to watch the children
When they find an Easter egg
They jump around for joy
and clap their little hands

So if you see the Easter bunny
Don't get in his way,
He's busy hiding Easter eggs
For this Easter day

The 4th of July

Let's honor all who fought or died to make America free
No better time than July 4th I'm sure we'll all agree
Let's remember Paul Revere a patriotic man
He rode to warn the settlers that the Brits
were close at hand
They fought the war for freedom
The settlers finally won
The settlers were determined
to get the red coats on the run
It was a job well done.
Let's honor all who keep America free
Cause everybody knows that freedom isn't free.

Halloween

Black cats and witches out after dark

Ghost and vampires out for a lark

This all happens on Halloween night

While all Jack O' Lanterns are burning so bright

Kids will be running from door to door

To get Caramel apples and candy galore

But ain't it such fun when trick or treats done

To go home and enjoy all the goodies.

Thanksgiving

When Thanksgiving is here
Let's give thanks for everything dear
Our family and friends
Our freedom and faith
And let's give thanks for the food on our plate
Roast turkey and dressing and cranberries too
Pumpkin pie for dessert and a long nap in view
After clean up is through
I'll kick off my shoes,
I'll sit by the fire and take a long snooze

Rudolph - Tiny snowflakes

Tiny little snowflakes
So pretty but so cold
You make the young so happy
The opposite for the old
The old get out their meds
The kids get out their sleds,
make snowmen, throw snowballs
There's lots of fun ahead
But let it snow on Christmas eve cause
Rudolph's raring to go
He waited patiently all year
So let it snow, let it snow, let it snow.

No little Child should hear

The fireplace is glowing the tree is all trimmed
Little Johnny is waiting for Santa to drop in
All of a sudden a knock on the door
It was jolly old Santa with packages galore
But ain't it a shame that Santa can't stay?
He has to get going with his reindeers and sleigh
Soon papa appears without the red suit and beard
He winks at mama and they both shed a tear
Santa has made little Johnny's heart glad
But Johnny doesn't know that papa is Santa
And Santa is dad.

Santa gets stuck

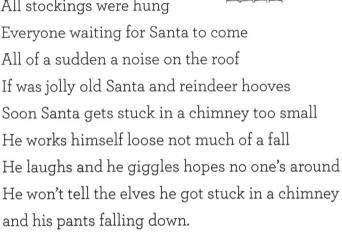

It was Christmas eve
All stockings were hung
Everyone waiting for Santa to come
All of a sudden a noise on the roof
If was jolly old Santa and reindeer hooves
Soon Santa gets stuck in a chimney too small
He works himself loose not much of a fall
He laughs and he giggles hopes no one's around
He won't tell the elves he got stuck in a chimney
and his pants falling down.

What every child should hear

Merry Christmas little kids,
Santa's almost here.
All kinds of excitement
at this wonderful time of the year.
The trees are all trimmed
and the packages too.
Santa's helpers
are ready for you.
But let's not forget
what Christmas is for,
to wish Happy Birthday
to the sweet baby Lord.

New Year's Eve

When it's New Year's eve
Let's start to celebrate
Let's make some resolutions
We'll try not to break
Let's be more kind
Let's lose some weight
Let's stop smoking for everyone's sake
There will be singing and dancing
Horn blowing and beer flowing
Drinkers take warning
If you've had a good time
But too much to drink
Better grab a cab
Go straight home and have a good sleep.

Made in United States
Troutdale, OR
07/09/2024

21110585R00043